The ***Loch Striven*** at Sconser. *(Brian Maxted)*

Caledonian

the fleet

Second Edition: March 1999

Compiled for Caledonian MacBrayne

by

Miles Cowsill, John Hendy & Lawrence Macduff

ISBN: 1 871947 55 3

Published by

PO Box 9, Narberth, Pembrokeshire, SA68 0YT.

TEL: +44 (0)1834 891460 FAX: +44 (0)1834) 891463

Foreword

I am delighted as the new incoming Managing Director to be asked to write this Foreword. In the last few years there have been a number of changes to the fleet. Older vessels, *Iona, Claymore, Suilven, Rhum, Morvern* and *Coll* have gone. New vessels, *Isle of Lewis, Loch Alainn, Loch Bhrusda* and *Clansman* have joined the fleet and the Kyle boats *Loch's Fyne* and *Dunvegan* have rejoined the fleet from lay up. On order for delivery in 2000/2001 is new tonnage to replace *Lochmor* and *Pioneer*.

Caledonian MacBrayne's prime purpose is the provision of essential passenger and cargo services to the islands off the West Coast of Scotland. The continuing and substantial investment in ships and shore facilities supports both the government's and the company's commitment to providing the very best service to the island communities and the tourists.

The scenery of the western seaboard of Scotland is both unique and spectacular, and whatever the weather the best way to see it, in all its moods, is from the deck of a Caledonian MacBrayne ferry.

This book describes the history of Caledonian MacBrayne and lists the current fleet in some detail for tourist and West Highland Steamer buff alike.

I wish the book every success and hope it will encourage those who read it to explore the islands and lochs of Scotland's West Coast.

John Simkins

Captain John Simkins
Managing Director

*The **Isle of Mull** leaving Craignure for Oban. (Miles Cowsill)*

The Caledonian MacBrayne Story

The name "Caledonian MacBrayne" is synonymous with sea travel to the coasts and islands of the West of Scotland. The Company operates a fleet of 27 modern roll on-roll off car and passenger ferries serving the Clyde estuary, the West Coast and the Western Isles. In all, their ships call at 51 different ports or terminals and serve some 22 islands.

The origins of the present Company extend back for no less than 150 years, but it was the creation of the Scottish Transport Group in 1969 which sets the scene for our story. The Group acquired the assets of the Caledonian Steam Packet Company Ltd. whose services mainly operated in the Clyde area. It also acquired the assets of David MacBrayne Ltd, whose operating area extended from Glasgow to the Outer Hebrides. In 1973, the operations of both Companies were merged with the formation of Caledonian MacBrayne Ltd. In 1990, ownership passed directly to the Secretary of State for Scotland, to whom Caledonian MacBrayne remain directly responsible.

The motor car has now been with us for 100 years, but only by the early 1950's had it started to become affordable to the general public. This increasing popularity resulted in the introduction of the first generation of vehicle-carrying ferries to the Clyde in 1954 and to the Western Isles in 1964. These ships all incorporated lifts which permitted the handling of vehicle traffic at either side of the ship at all states of the tide. Minimal alteration was required to existing pier structures except for some localised strengthening to cope with the greater weights being handled. The new ships brought increased accessibility to the coasts and islands they served and traffic carried grew with remarkable regularity. This soon underlined the requirement not only for larger ferries but also for a far

The veteran turbine excursion steamer ***King George V*** at Oban's North Pier in June 1973. *(John Hendy)*

The ***Jupiter*** seen arriving at Largs dressed overall. *(David Parsons)*

quicker method of embarking and discharging vehicles. A typical hoist could carry six cars but the time taken to manoeuvre them on and off the lift together with the inherent slowness in lift operation soon caused unacceptable delays.

Elsewhere the standard method of loading vehicles on board ferries had been by the stern through entrances specially fitted with watertight doors. These end-loading ferries used purpose-built terminals and linkspans, ramps connecting ship with shore, were constructed to allow both a constant flow of traffic and a better service frequency. More recent designs used doors at each end and this improved system was adopted by David MacBrayne Ltd. for their new ship, which was under construction at Troon late in 1969. At the same time, the Norwegian-built *Stena Baltica*, another ship of this type, was acquired second hand by the Scottish Transport Group. Though only three years old, she underwent a major refit at Greenock and, as the *Caledonia*, she pioneered drive-through operations on the Arran link at the start of the summer of 1970. The modernised service was an instant success.

The conversion of the Arran service was the precursor of a far-ranging modernisation programme. David MacBrayne's new ship, the *Iona*, was additionally fitted with a lift and this dual capability allowed the use of the ship virtually everywhere in the service network. This element of flexibility was very necessary while the

The car ferry ***Bute*** leaving Dunoon. *(Andrew Jones)*

The ***Pioneer*** arriving at Mallaig. *(David Parsons)*

programme of route conversions was in hand. The *Iona* was intended for the Islay service to whose indigenous distillery traffic she was well suited, but for various reasons it was a rival company who got there first when in 1967 their new ro-ro ship *Sound of Islay* entered service. The *Iona's* flexibility allowed her to operate on the Gourock - Dunoon service initially thus releasing the pioneer Clyde car ferry *Arran* for the job of converting the Islay service to a vehicle ferry operation in competition.

The challenges for the new Scottish Transport Group were immense. The Arran service had been successfully upgraded but now the island of Skye was calling for attention. The Caledonian Steam Packet's outpost at Kyle of Lochalsh employed five small side- loading craft for the short crossing to Kyleakin. Three of these ships were less than ten years old but it was clear that larger ferries were urgently required. As a result, orders were placed for two ferries of drive-through design for the Kyle of Lochalsh-Kyleakin route and the first, named *Kyleakin*, was delivered in 1970. She could carry 28 cars, four times as many as any of the small craft previously used. In the fleet, she was revolutionary in that she was fitted with the well-tried Voith Schneider propulsion system which gave her the outstanding manoeuvrability much needed in these tidal waters. Her sistership *Lochalsh* joined her in 1971 and both ferries enjoyed intensive twenty-year careers before larger craft replaced them. As for the redundant vessels, new work was soon found for them.

The ***Columba*** departing from the North Pier, Oban. *(John Hendy)*

The ***Suilven*** at Ullapool in July 1991. *(J R Clague)*

The fairly new *Portree* and *Broadford* were converted to bow loaders for the Colintraive - Rhubodach (Bute) crossing and continued in service for another fifteen years. The *Coruisk* was also converted to bow loading and launched a new route from Largs to Cumbrae Slip. Such was her success that later that year the old *Kyleakin*, was similarly converted and renamed *Largs*. The fifth craft, *Lochalsh*, was renamed *Scalpay* and replaced a small turntable ferry on the crossing between Harris and her namesake island. It was as important to upgrade the small ferry links as it was for the major routes, for those crossings were also vital to the communities they served.

Another new service commenced during 1972 linking Lochranza on Arran's north west coast and Claonaig on the Kintyre peninsula. This route was aimed at attracting seasonal tourist traffic and the *Kilbrannan*, the first of a new class of eight small bow-loading craft, was detailed for the job. The link again proved a success and her seven Island class sisters went on to pioneer many other new services.

Early in 1973, the newly merged companies under the Caledonian MacBrayne banner adopted a common livery. Black hulls remained standard but the red funnel of the David MacBrayne lineage was now carried with the lion rampant emblem on the yellow disc background of the former Caledonian Steam Packet Company. Initially the house flag was that of David MacBrayne with the yellow circle and lion but in June 1980, the flag was changed

The ***Iona*** arriving at Armadale (Skye). *(Miles Cowsill)*

The ***Hebridean Isles*** at Uig (Skye). *(Miles Cowsill)*

The ***Isle of Arran*** arriving at Ardrossan in June 1990. *(Ferry Publications Library)*

again to reflect the new funnel design.

Developments this year saw the cessation of the lengthy Mallaig - Kyle - Stornoway (Lewis) passenger and cargo service. Using the shortest crossing philosophy, the mainland base now became Ullapool and the service was converted to drive-through. As a temporary measure until a new ship could be obtained, the decision was made to convert the second of the 1964 trio of side loading Hebridean ferries. The *Clansman's* reconstruction at Troon was a major exercise and until she was ready, the ubiquitous *Iona* inaugurated the new service. Once freed by the new-look *Clansman*, the *Iona* was transferred to Oban to relieve the hard-pressed former Clyde ferry *Bute* on the crossing to Mull.

Another new service which became operational during the 1973 season was that across the Sound of Mull between Lochaline (on the Morvern coast) and the new Mull terminal at Fishnish. The Island class vessel *Morvern* commenced the service but was soon to be superseded by sister vessel *Bruernish*. The *Morvern* in turn went to Oban to convert the Lismore route for vehicle use.

The final major development of the year was the launch at Port Glasgow of a new ship for the Gourock - Dunoon service. Here, as elsewhere, side loading operation had demonstrated its limitations but the solution here departed from normal practice in that the new ship, *Jupiter*, was fitted with both a stern ramp and a pair of side ramps. She entered service in spring 1974 and berthed stern-first at Gourock while at Dunoon she discharged her traffic by her starboard side ramp onto a linkspan set into the face of the pier. Equipped with Voith Schneider propulsion units fore and aft, the *Jupiter's* unrivalled manoeuvrability allowed her to maintain an hourly service from each terminal with minimal turn-round times. As her running mate she had the former passenger ferry *Maid of Cumbrae* which had been neatly converted in 1972 using the same combination of stern and side ramps.

The *Glen Sannox*, the 1957-built former Arran ferry which had herself been converted to stern loading in 1970, had spent much of her subsequent career on both the Rothesay (Bute) and Dunoon runs but was now released to take over the Oban - Craignure (Mull) link in 1974. Her period of duty there was to be brief as the *Clansman* was later freed from Ullapool to serve on the route. For the Ullapool-Stornoway run, the Company had acquired the new Norwegian-built ferry *Suilven*. Very much the state of the art vessel for her time, she set new standards for the Lewis service and was to remain there for virtually her entire career.

The *Iona* was as busy as ever when, during 1974, she was transferred to work the long haul from Oban out to Barra and South Uist, bringing vehicle ferry operation to those islands. The first step in bringing this route to full drive-through working occurred that summer with the opening of the linkspan at Lochboisdale (South Uist). At the end of this first season, the *Iona* was refitted and provided with the necessary sleeping berths for her new crossing.

Yet another major event took place that autumn when a new ship took over the Islay route from the former Clyde ferry, *Arran*. The *Pioneer*, a product of the Robb Caledon yard at Leith, was not of drive-through design but used her stern ramp at both terminals.

A sister ship for the *Jupiter*, the *Juno*, joined the Gourock - Dunoon route in December 1974.

Yet another new service was launched in 1975. Linking Portree in Skye with the island of Raasay, the *Eigg* - the sixth of the Island class ferries- inaugurated the route but was replaced during the following spring by the seventh

The Island class vessel ***Bruernish*** at Oban. *(Brian Maxted)*

The Island class vessel ***Eigg*** crossing Oban Bay. *(John Hendy)*

vessel, *Canna*, when the Skye terminal changed from Portree to the new slipway at Sconser. The final ship of the series was aptly named *Raasay* and became the route's permanent incumbent.

The Arran ferry *Caledonia*, having enjoyed six hectic and busy summers, had by this stage become a victim of her own success and so was moved to Oban in exchange for the larger *Clansman*. The *Caledonia* returned to Arran each winter, but at Oban either the *Glen Sannox* or the *Arran* took the winter sailings.

Vehicle traffic on the Largs - Cumbrae Slip service also continued to expand and required the assistance of an Island class vessel before the new drive-through ferry *Isle of Cumbrae* appeared in the spring of 1977.

It was now the turn of the island of Bute to receive improvements. Up until this time the side-loaders *Cowal* and *Glen Sannox* had been the mainstay of the service and the latter vessel had inaugurated linkspan loading during 1977. However, in the following year a third vessel of the *Jupiter* class - the *Saturn* - took up the Rothesay route.

One of the ever versatile Island class commenced serving on the Harris to Scalpay crossing during 1977. Initially using the *Morvern* working from Tarbert, the *Kilbrannan* later became the regular ship, latterly operating from an improved slipway at Kyles Scalpay.

In 1979, the *Iona* finally took over the Islay service for which she was intended and operated from a recently acquired site at Kennacraig, further down West Loch Tarbert, where access for a ship of her size was possible. Kennacraig also accommodated the temporary operation of the Gigha service using the *Bruernish* until the new slipway at Tayinloan, further south on the Kintyre coast, was opened in 1980. The new crossing only took 20 minutes and permitted a far better frequency of sailings than had hitherto been possible. Gigha and Islay had until 1979 been served by one ship but now the *Iona* was able to devote her full attention to Islay and calls at Port Askaig, in the north east of the island, were resumed after an absence of several years.

The transfer of the *Iona* to Islay was facilitated by the

The ***Lochmor*** seen in Mallaig harbour. *(David Parsons)*

The ***Hebridean Isles*** arriving at Uig. *(Miles Cowsill)*

The ***Isle of Cumbrae*** pictured loading at Rhubodach. *(Brian Maxted)*

delivery of the new Leith-built *Claymore* - a name first used by MacBrayne's in 1881 and only recently relinquished by the previous ship of that name. She had been built in 1955 for the Oban, Coll, Tiree, Barra and South Uist services and now the new vessel perpetuated the historic name on these links.

The 'Sacred Isle' of Iona became served by the much-travelled *Morvern* which in 1979 replaced the small flotilla of open boats known affectionately as 'the red boats', which had been a feature of this service for many years. But while the *Morvern* brought vehicle carrying capacity to the run, it was only for the use of island residents as it was feared that large numbers of tourists' cars would spoil the timeless appeal of the island.

The ***Caledonian Isles*** seen shortly after her launch.

The ***Isle of Arran*** at Port Askaig with the Paps of Jura behind. *(Brian Maxted)*

Another new ship from the Ailsa yard at Troon arrived on station during 1979 in the form of the passenger ferry *Lochmor*. She was built for the Small Isles service and is the only pure passenger/ cargo vessel in the present fleet. An Island class vessel was impractical on the exposed run from Mallaig out to the sparsely populated islands of Rum, Eigg, Muck and Canna and so the new vessel was considered as the most cost effective design for serving the archipelago.

Traffic on the Arran route continued to rise and in 1983 the Ferguson Ailsa yard at Port Glasgow had construction of the new *Isle of Arran* in hand. She commenced her duties in April 1984 and set new standards of capacity and comfort which all later vessels were to follow. The ship was an immediate success but just nine years later she was to make way for an even larger ship : so history repeats itself. During the previous year, the Company had adopted the marketing ploy of advertising its name in bold white lettering on the black hulls of most of the fleet. The *Isle of Arran* was the first new ship to carry this feature, while the Island class carried the legend in black on their mainly white hulls.

Back in 1964, a triangular vehicle ferry service had been established between Skye, Harris and North Uist using the *Hebrides* - the first of the trio of side loading ferries for service in the Western Isles. Its popularity and mounting delays caused by overwhelming summer traffic caused a basic rethink of the well-tried system of loading and by summer 1985 a new drive-through ferry was under construction by Cochrane Shipbuilders at Selby. Named *Hebridean Isles*, she was of similar dimensions to the *Isle of Arran* but was fitted with a lift so that she could be used elsewhere within the current service network if the need arose. She was internally fitted out to the highest standards, upholding the tradition of her predecessor. The *Hebridean Isles* and her new terminals were the first to be built with financial assistance from the European Community.

The short crossings operated by the Island class vessels also became victims of the increasing traffic volumes and

The ***Lord of the Isles*** nearing Oban. *(Caledonian MacBrayne)*

new tonnage was the only satisfactory answer. In 1986, four new vessels which became known as the 'Loch' class were built by Dunston of Hessle. Following their long delivery voyages up the east coast to Inverness, they passed through the Caledonian Canal before taking up their duties: the *Loch Linnhe* and *Loch Striven* at Largs (Cumbrae service), the *Loch Riddon* at Colintraive (for the secondary link with Bute) and, in 1987, the *Loch Ranza* at Claonaig (for the secondary route to Arran). On the latter two routes, drive-through facilities were introduced for the first time. These vessels have no funnels but their wheelhouses were painted red with a black top, a nice touch which improved their overall appearance. With new ships on the Cumbrae crossing, the *Isle of Cumbrae* was moved to the Lochaline - Fishnish link across the Sound of Mull. All the former Kyle ferries were sold, and displaced Island class vessels were found other work. The *Coll* was used in 1986 to take over the summer service between Tobermory (Mull) and Mingary on the Ardnamurchan peninsula - the western-most point on the British mainland.

By 1987, the pioneer drive-through ship *Caledonia* was experiencing similar capacity problems to those previously seen elsewhere within the fleet. At the end of the year her replacement was launched at Port Glasgow and was the largest and most impressive ferry yet. Aptly named *Isle of Mull*, the new vessel commenced service from Oban to Craignure (Mull) in 1988 and incorporated sailings to the island of Colonsay which received its linkspan in the same year.

At this time another new vessel was taking shape on the stocks at Port Glasgow and was launched as the *Lord of the Isles* in March 1989. Ready to enter service in late May, the new ship replaced the *Claymore* on the Barra and South Uist service from Oban. Her appearance resembled that of the *Isle of Mull* in that she had the same fully enclosed bridge but her profile bore distinct similarities to the *Hebridean Isles* as the new ship incorporated a lift. Fitted out to the same high standards as her Mull and Skye consorts, she had the additional power and speed needed to maintain the exacting

The ***Loch Linnhe*** leaving Cumbrae for Largs. *(Brian Maxted)*

The ***Loch Tarbert*** at Lochranza (Arran). *(Brian Maxted)*

schedule on not just the Barra and South Uist service but also the Coll and Tiree run which was incorporated into her roster. The linkspan at Castlebay (Barra) came into use that summer completing drive- through operations on this service but Coll and Tiree still required use of the vessel's side hoist until 1992.

Having completed ten years of faithful service to the Outer Isles, the *Claymore* was given a thorough internal refurbishment to bring her up to the standards of her newer fleet companions. Thus revitalised, she replaced the smaller *Iona* on the Islay service. She also revived the link from Islay to Oban via Colonsay in the summer.

The *Iona* now moved to the seasonal service linking Mallaig and Armadale, on Skye. The route had been opened in 1964 using the then new *Clansman* and she was followed by her sister-ship *Columba* (1973-74), the former Clyde ferry *Bute* (1975-78) and from 1979 the *Pioneer* had transferred here from Islay. A side lift had been fitted for this purpose but, now that she had been freed from the Mallaig station, she sailed south to the Clyde again where fixed side ramps were installed to replace the lift. She then supplemented the services of the *Jupiter*, *Juno* and *Saturn* as required. Once again, this interchangeability can be seen to play a major role in maximising the deployment of the fleet as requirements dictate in the network.

Following the decision taken in 1988 to privatise the Scottish Bus Group, the road transport arm of the

The ***Isle of Mull*** arriving at Oban. *(Colin J. Smith)*

Scottish Transport Group, consideration was then given to privatising Caledonian MacBrayne Ltd. It was however decided to leave the Company in public ownership which passed directly to the Secretary of State for Scotland during 1990. A new Board of Directors was formed in readiness to take the Company forward into its third decade of development.

Twenty years on from the conversion of the Kyle of Lochalsh - Kyleakin (Skye) crossing to drive-through operation, attention was once more focused on the service. Orders were placed with Fergusons at Port Glasgow for a larger pair of ships which were updated versions of those which they replaced. Named *Loch Dunvegan* and *Loch Fyne* they were delivered during 1991. When the Skye bridge was completed in October 1995 they were offered for sale and were eventually brought back into the fleet during autumn 1997.

By the end of 1991, plans were afoot to expand the 'Loch' class to provide further service enhancements. As a result, two new ships were delivered in the summer of 1992 from the Miller yard in St. Monans, Fife. The first to arrive was the *Loch Buie* which was designed specifically for the Iona service. The route carries large numbers of coach-borne foot passengers and with this in mind, she is far more of a passenger carrier than other members of the class. The second ship was named *Loch Tarbert* and took over the Lochranza - Claonaig service on which a larger ferry was already needed. The previous resident, the *Loch Ranza*, was accordingly transferred to the Gigha route.

The next development again harks back to the start of this evolutionary process. Arran's popularity as a holiday destination has held-up over many years. Had this not been the case then there would have been no need to replace the *Isle of Arran* so soon after her introduction but it was clearly becoming necessary as even she was unable to handle all the available traffic on offer at peak times. As a result, August 1993 saw the newly delivered *Caledonian Isles* proudly sail up the Clyde from her birthplace at Richards' yard at Lowestoft. The first of the

The ***Loch Riddon*** seen departing from Largs. *(Brian Maxted)*

The ***Caledonian Isles*** berthed at Brodick. *(Colin J. Smith)*

Company's ships ever to exceed 5,000 gross tons, and in length greater than any previous ship built for the Clyde or Western Isles services, she is a design development of the *Isle of Mull* with even more spacious accommodation for passengers and 50% more vehicle deck space for cars than her predecessor.

The entry into service of the new ship saw the *Isle of Arran* transferred to Islay where her extra capacity has allowed further growth in traffic.

The evolution of the fleet, as briefly outlined within these pages, is a never-ending process. The joint venture with the Isle of Man Steam Packet Company between 1994-96 saw the *Claymore* making regular weekly summer sailings to Douglas until she was purchased by Sea Containers in 1997 for their subsidiary company the Argyll & Antrim Steam Packet Company to operate the summer service linking Campbeltown and Ballycastle. At the Co. Antrim port she joined the Island class ferry *Canna* which had been transferred to the new service linking Ballycastle with Rathlin Island in spring 1997. The *Canna* was one of a number of ferries which had been used on the service to Scalpay which was closed following the construction of a bridge to Harris in 1997.

A new short ferry crossing was introduced in 1994 initially using the *Rhum* linking Tarbert (Loch Fyne), with Portavadie on the other side of the loch, and such was its success that by 1998 a larger 'Loch' class ferry had been transferred to the route which had become year-round.

*The **Loch Fyne** seen at Lochaline. (Brian Maxted)*

1999 – Isle of Cumbrae introduced. Since 1996 the short link between North Uist and Harris across the Sound of Harris has given local people and visitors much more convenient access between these islands using the new *Loch Bhrusda*. The seasonal service between Mallaig and Armadale (Skye) was upgraded in spring 1994 to a full ro-ro service - these were the last two piers in the west of Scotland to be modernised. Two new vehicle routes were also opened in 1994 between Rothesay and Brodick (closed at the end of the 1998 season) and linking Mallaig with Lochboisdale and Castlebay.

The arrival of the Port Glasgow built *Isle of Lewis* to

replace the twenty-year-old *Suilven* on the Stornoway-Lewis link during late 1995 cut an hour from the crossing of the Minch while offering improved standards of comfort and the entry into service of the new *Clansman* in July 1998 provided the islanders of Coll, Tiree, Barra and South Uist with the latest in luxury. The year 1999 sees the the Company's largest ferry make a Sunday call at Colonsay in addition to her other commitments. As CalMac's latest vessel took up service from Oban, the *Lord of the Isles* was switched to the summer services from Mallaig while the faithful *Iona* had been retired and sold to Orkney owners at the close of her 1997 season.

In early 1999 the company announced plans to build two new ferries. The first contact worth £5.5m, is to build a new vessel for the Mallaig-Small Isles to carry 200 passengers and 14 cars to replace the *Lochmor*. The second new ship will placed on the Skye/Harris/North Uist routes and will have capacity for 650 passengers and 110 cars and will be of similar design to that of the *Clansman;* the new ship will replace the *Pioneer*. Both vessels are due enter service during the year 2000 .

The special feature of the Caledonian MacBrayne operation is the serving of remote communities. The majority of these routes are not, nor are they ever likely to be, profit-making undertakings. This was much apparent as far back as 70 years ago. What CalMac has been conspicuously successful in doing is reducing the amount of State support required in real terms, over a

Caledonian MacBrayne's ***Clansman*** leaving Oban for the Outer Hebrides. *(Brian Maxted)*

period of many years. The entire programme of modernisation described here has been a major factor in this achievement. It has allowed the more efficient use of capital assets together with a streamlining and improvement of the services provided. The Company has also become more aggressive in marketing itself to the tourist industry. In the eyes of a large majority of people whose lives are materially affected, the quality of service provided by Caledonian MacBrayne is held in high regard.

The ***Isle of Lewis*** berthed at Ullapool. *(Colin J. Smith)*

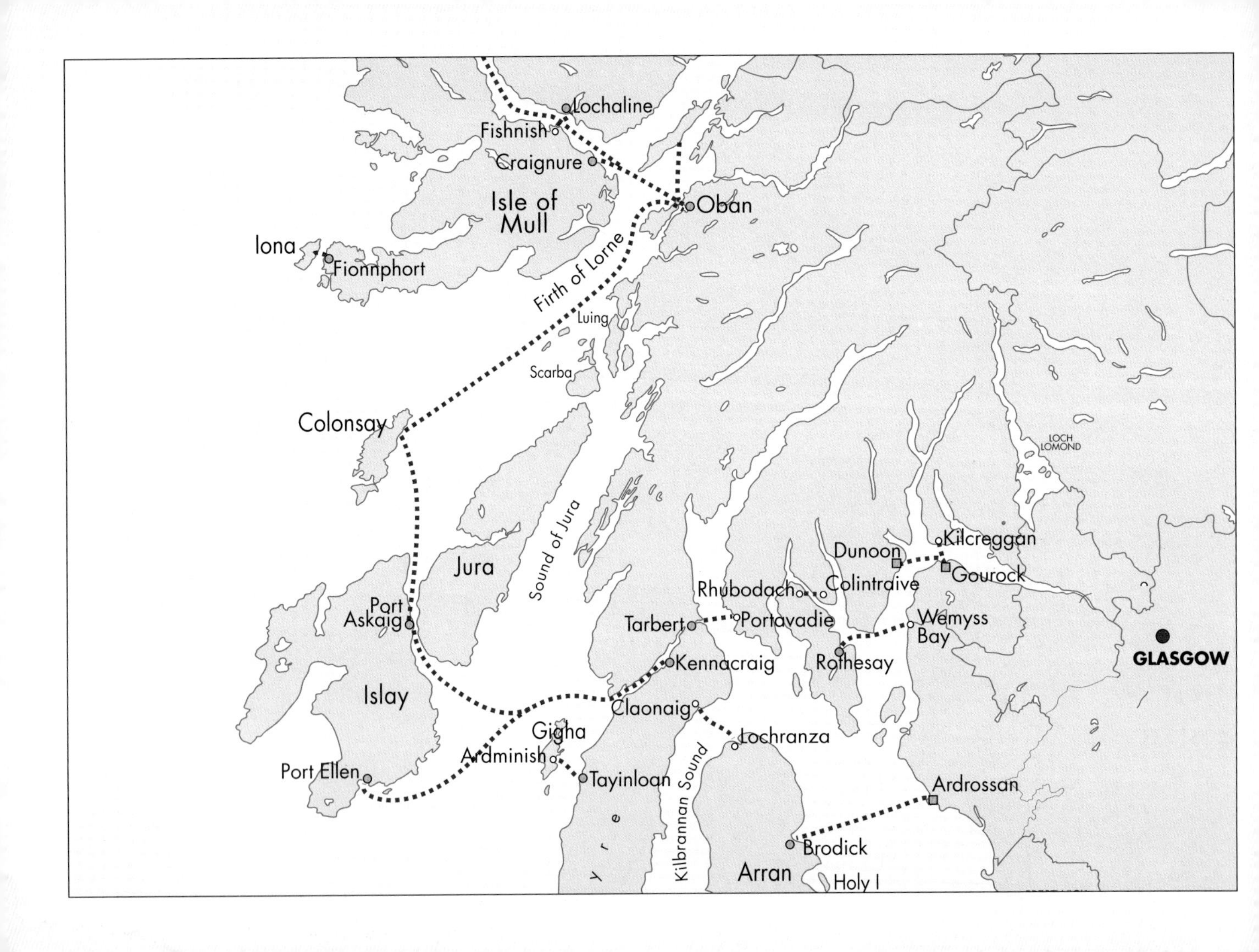

Lochaline
Fishnish
Craignure
Isle of Mull
Oban
Iona
Fionnphort
Firth of Lorne
Luing
Scarba
Colonsay
LOCH LOMOND
Sound of Jura
Jura
Kilcreggan
Dunoon
Gourock
Rhubodach
Colintraive
Port Askaig
Tarbert
Portavadie
Wemyss Bay
Kennacraig
Rothesay
GLASGOW
Islay
Claonaig
Gigha
Lochranza
Ardminish
Port Ellen
Tayinloan
Kilbrannan Sound
Ardrossan
Brodick
Arran
Holy I

Ferry Routes of Caledonian MacBrayne

The ***Rhum*** at Kilchoan. *(Brian Maxted)*

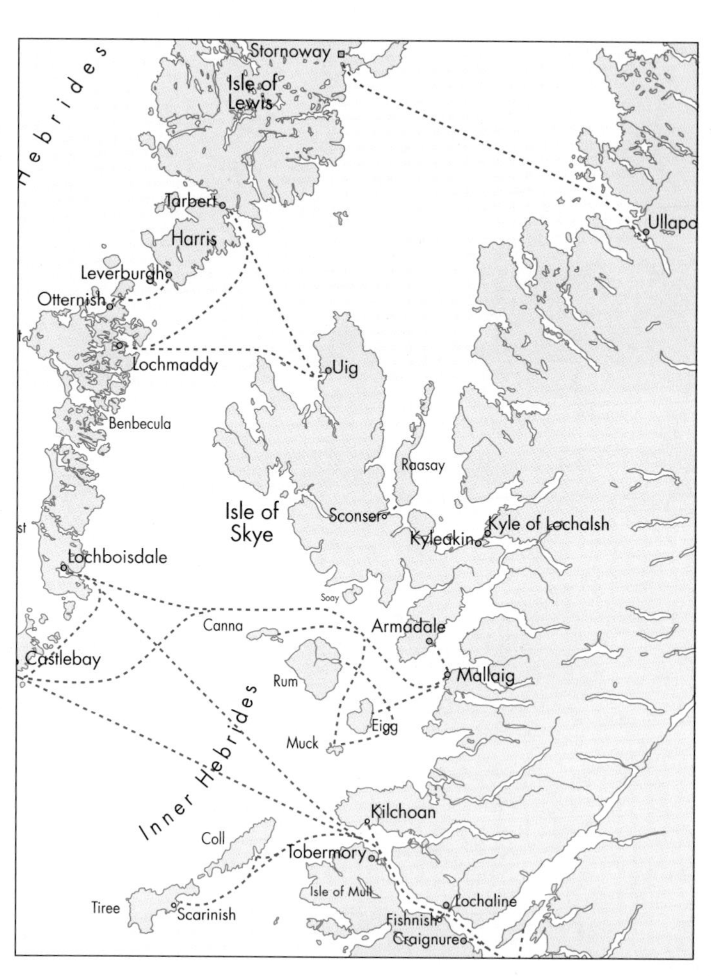

The ***Clansman*** and the ***Lord of the Isles*** at Oban's Railway pier in July 1998. *(Caledonian MacBrayne)*

PIERS AND TERMINALS USED BY CALEDONIAN MACBRAYNE

Pier	Owner
Gourock	CalMac
Kilcreggan	Strathclyde Regional Council
Dunoon	Strathclyde Regional Council
Wemyss Bay	CalMac
Rothesay	Strathclyde Regional Council (CalMac's own linkspan)
Colintraive	CalMac
Rhubodach	CalMac
Tarbert (Loch Fyne)	Tarbert Harbour Authority
Portavadie	Argyll & Isles Enterprise
Largs	CalMac
Cumbrae Slip	CalMac
Ardrossan	Ardrossan Harbour Company/Clyde Port
Brodick	CalMac
Claonaig	CalMac
Lochranza	CalMac
Tighnabruaich	Strathclyde Regional Council
Kennacraig	CalMac
Port Ellen	CalMac
Port Askaig	Strathclyde Regional Council

The ***Lord of the Isles*** and ***Lochmor*** at Mallaig with Eigg behind. *(Brian Maxted)*

Pier	Owner
Tayinloan	Strathclyde Regional Council
Gigha	Strathclyde Regional Council
Oban (Railway Pier)	CalMac
Lismore	Strathclyde Regional Council
Colonsay	CalMac
Craignure	Strathclyde Regional Council
Lochaline	CalMac
Fishnish	CalMac
Fionnphort	Strathclyde Regional Council

Pier	Owner
Iona	Strathclyde Regional Council
Tobermory	CalMac
Kilchoan	CalMac
Coll	CalMac
Tiree	CalMac
Mallaig	Mallaig Harbour Authority
Eigg	Isle of Eigg Trust
Muck	Laurence McEwan
Rum	Scottish Natural Heritage
Canna	National Trust for Scotland
Armadale	CalMac
Raasay	Highland Regional Council
Castlebay	CalMac
Lochboisdale	CalMac
Uig	Highland Regional Council
Tarbert (Harris)	CalMac
Lochmaddy	Western Isles Council
Otternish (N.Uist)	Western Isles Council
Leverburgh (Harris)	Western Isles Council
Ullapool	Ullapool Pier Trustees
Stornoway	Stornoway Pier & Harbour Commission

The ***Saturn*** arriving at Dunoon. *(John Hendy)*

the **fleet**

The ***Lord of the Isles*** *passing Innellan*

CALEDONIAN ISLES

Brian Maxted

Built	1993
Builders	Richards Shipbuilders, Lowestoft
Gross tons	5,221
Nett tons	1,566
Deadweight	7,66.7
Length	94.0m
Breadth	15.8m
Draught	3.2m
Speed	15 kts
Passengers	1000
Crew	26
Cars	110
Ro-Ro (m)	150m
Call Sign	MRAB8

ISLE OF MULL

Miles Cowsill

Built	1988
Builders	Appledore Ferguson Ltd., Port Glasgow
Gross tons	4,719
Net tons	1,415
Deadweight	592
Length	90.03m
Breadth	15.8m
Draught	3.19m
Speed	15 kts
Passengers (max)	1000
Crew (max)	28
Cars	80
Ro-Ro (m)	150m
Call Sign	MJCEC

HEBRIDEAN ISLES

Miles Cowsill

Built	1985
Builders	Cochrane Shipbuilders Ltd., Selby
Gross tons	3,040
Nett tons	912
Deadweight	671
Length	85.15m
Breadth	15.8m
Draught	3.11m
Speed	15 kts
Passengers	507
Crew	24
Cars	68
Ro-Ro (m)	150m
Call Sign	GFMJ

ISLE OF LEWIS

Colin J. Smith

Built	1995
Builders	Ferguson Shipbuilders Ltd, Port Glasgow
Gross tons	6,753
Nett tons	2,025
Deadweight	867
Length	101.25m
Breadth	18.52m
Draught	4.19m
Speed	18 kts
Passengers	680
Crew	32
Cars	123
Ro-Ro (m)	240m
Call Sign	MVNP4

ISLE OF ARRAN

Brian Maxted

Built	1984
Builders	Ferguson Ailsa Ltd., Port Glasgow
Gross tons	3,296
Nett tons	988
Deadweight	666
Length	84.9m
Breadth	15.8m
Draught	3.2m
Speed	15 kts
Passengers	448
Crew	20
Cars	76
Ro-Ro (m)	120m
Call Sign	GDMJ

LORD OF THE ISLES

Built	1989
Builders	Appledore Ferguson Ltd., Port Glasgow
Gross tons	3,504
Nett tons	1,051
Deadweight	464
Length	84.6m
Breadth	15.8m
Draught	3.19m
Speed	16 kts
Passengers	506
Crew	28
Cars	56
Ro-Ro (m)	130m
Call Sign	MKHA7

CLANSMAN

Caledonian MacBrayne

Built	1998
Builders	Appledore Shipbuilders Ltd., North Devon
Gross tons	5,400
Nett tons	1,800
Deadweight	600
Length	99.0m
Breadth	15.8m
Draught	3.22m
Speed	16.5 kts
Passengers	634
Crew	32
Cars	90
Ro-Ro (m)	170m
Call Sign	MXX98

PIONEER

Lawrence Macduff

Built	1974
Builders	Robb Caledon Shipbuilders Ltd., Leith
Gross tons	1,071
Nett tons	358
Deadweight	142
Length	67m
Breadth	13.4m
Draught	2.4m
Speed	16 kts
Passengers (max)	356
Crew	21
Cars	32
Ro-Ro (m)	50m
Call Sign	GULA

JUNO

Lawrence Macduff

Built	1974
Builders	James Lamont & Co. Ltd., Port Glasgow
Gross tons	853.71
Nett tons	304.14
Deadweight	261
Length	66.45m
Breadth	13.8m
Draught	2.45m
Speed	12 kts
Passengers	510
Crew	10
Cars	40
Ro-Ro (m)	60m
Call Sign	GUMS

JUPITER

Built	1974
Builders	James Lamont & Co. Ltd., Port Glasgow
Gross tons	848.61
Nett tons	306.10
Deadweight	247
Length	66.45m
Breadth	13.8m
Draught	2.45m
Speed	12 kts
Passengers	510
Crew	10
Cars	40
Ro-Ro (m)	60m
Call Sign	GUIF

SATURN

Lawrence Macduff

Built	1978
Builders	Ailsa Shipbuilding Co. Ltd., Troon
Gross tons	851.26
Nett tons	302.87
Deadweight	247
Length	69.5m
Breadth	13.8m
Draught	2.45m
Speed	12 kts
Passengers	510
Crew	10
Cars	40
Ro-Ro (m)	60m
Call Sign	GXID

LOCH DUNVEGAN

Brian Maxted

Built	1991
Builders	Ferguson Shipbuilders Ltd., Port Glasgow
Gross tons	549
Nett tons	170
Deadweight	190
Length	54.2m
Breadth	13.0m
Draught	1.6m
Speed	9 kts
Passengers	250
Crew	4
Cars	36
Ro-Ro (m)	100m
Call Sign	MNFE3

LOCH FYNE

Brian Maxted

Built	1991
Builders	Ferguson Shipbuilders Ltd., Port Glasgow
Gross tons	549
Nett tons	170
Deadweight	190
Length	54.2m
Breadth	13.0m
Draught	1.6m
Speed	9 kts
Passengers	250
Crew	4
Cars	36
Ro-Ro (m)	100m
Call Sign	MNFF3

LOCHMOR

Built	1979
Builders	Ailsa Shipbuilding Co. Ltd., Troon
Gross tons	189
Nett tons	68.26
Deadweight	51
Length	30.98m
Breadth	8.01m
Draught	1.7m
Speed	10 kts
Passengers (max)	130
Crew	6
Cars	Nil
Call Sign	GYOR

ISLE OF CUMBRAE

Miles Cowsill

Built	1977
Builders	Ailsa Shipbuilding Co. Ltd., Troon
Gross tons	201
Nett tons	90.37
Deadweight	72
Length	32.0m
Breadth	10.0m
Draught	1.4m
Speed	8.5 kts
Passengers (max)	160
Crew	3
Cars	18
Ro-Ro (m)	52m
Call Sign	2MTM

LOCH BHRUSDA

Miles Cowsill

Built	1996
Builders	McTay Marine, Bromborough
Gross tons	246
Nett tons	80
Deadweight	80
Length	35.4m
Breadth	10.88m
Draught	1.4m
Speed	8 kts
Passengers (max)	150
Crew	3
Cars	18
Ro-Ro (m)	34m
Call Sign	MVFP9

LOCH LINNHE | LOCH RANZA | LOCH RIDDON | LOCH STRIVEN

Built	1986-87
Builders	Richard Dunston (Hessle) Ltd.
Gross tons	206
Nett tons	77
Deadweight	60
Length	30.2m
Breadth	10.0m
Draught	1.5m
Speed	9 kts
Passengers (max)	203
Crew	3
Cars	12
Ro-Ro (m)	30m
Call Signs	

LOCH LINNHE	MEXRG
LOCH RANZA	GJGJ
LOCH RIDDON	MFNN7
LOCH STRIVEN	MESXG

Loch Linnhe

Loch Riddon

LOCH BUIE

Brian Maxted

Built	1992
Builders	J W Miller & Sons Ltd., St Monans
Gross tons	295
Nett tons	105
Deadweight	62.7
Length	30.2m
Breadth	10.0m
Draught	1.6m
Speed	9 kts
Passengers (max)	250
Crew	4
Cars	10
Ro-Ro (m)	16m
Call Sign	MPJU9

LOCH TARBERT

Brian Maxted

Built	1992
Builders	J W Miller & Sons Ltd., St Monans
Gross tons	211
Nett tons	72
Deadweight	62
Length	30.2m
Breadth	10.0m
Draught	1.6m
Speed	9 kts
Passengers	150
Crew	3
Cars	18
Ro-Ro (m)	30m
Call Sign	MPJT9

LOCH ALAINN

Brian Maxted

Built	1997
Builders	Buckie Shipyard Ltd
Gross tons	396
Nett tons	125
Deadweight	128.5
Length	41m
Breadth	13.4m
Draught	1.73m
Speed	10.13 kts
Passengers	150
Crew	4
Cars	24
Ro-Ro (m)	34m
Call Sign	MX2G2

BRUERNISH

Built	1973
Builders	James Lamont & Co. Ltd., Port Glasgow
Gross tons	69
Nett tons	34
Deadweight	32.5
Length	22.5m
Breadth	6.4m
Draught	1.4m
Speed	8 kts
Passengers (max)	164
Crew	3
Cars	6
Ro-Ro (m)	13.5m
Call Sign	2CBV

EIGG

Miles Cowsill

Built	1975
Builders	James Lamont & Co. Ltd., Port Glasgow
Gross tons	69
Nett tons	34
Deadweight	32.5
Length	22.5m
Breadth	6.4m
Draught	1.4m
Speed	8 kts
Passengers (max)	164
Crew	3
Cars	5
Ro-Ro (m)	13.5m
Call Sign	2GFZ

RAASAY

Miles Cowsill

Built	1976
Builders	James Lamont & Co. Ltd., Port Glasgow
Gross tons	69
Nett tons	34
Deadweight	32.5
Length	22.5m
Breadth	6.4m
Draught	1.4m
Speed	8 kts
Passengers (max)	164
Crew	3
Cars	6
Ro-Ro (m)	13.5m
Call Sign	2IUC

CANNA

Lawrence Macduff

Built	1973
Builders	James Lamont & Co. Ltd., Port Glasgow
Gross tons	69
Nett tons	34
Deadweight	32.5
Length	22.5m
Breadth	6.4m
Draught	1.4m
Speed	8
Passengers (max)	164
Crew	3
Cars	6
Ro-Ro (m)	13.5m
Call Sign	2CBV

NOTES & ACKNOWLEDGEMENTS

The ***Lord of the Isles*** leaving Oban.

NOTES

1. In addition to the listed ships there is one motor launch, the ***Ulva***.
2. Ro-Ro (m) refers to vehicle deck space of sufficient headroom to accommodate lorry traffic.

ACKNOWLEDGEMENTS

The publishers would like to express their sincere gratitude to all those gentlemen who contributed towards this book. Special thanks are due to Mike Blair, Caledonian MacBrayne's Marketing Manager for all his assistance. Colin J. Smith, Brian Maxted, Dick Clague and David Parsons are also thanked for their input.